SCIENCE **DISCOVERY** TIMELINES

KEY DISCOVERIES IN
PHYSiCAL
SCiENCE

KATIE **MARSICO**

LERNER PUBLICATIONS ◆ MINNEAPOLIS

TO MY KIDS, MARIA, C. J., THOMAS, MEGAN, AND ABBY; MY MOM, ANN KONRATH; MY HUSBAND, CARL MARSICO; AND MY PHENOMENAL BABYSITTER AND FRIEND, ANGELA GRABENHOFER

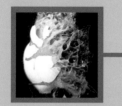

cover image
In 1612 astronomer and physicist Galileo Galilei first explained the concept of inertia. Inertia is a property of matter by which an object, such as this ball of paint, stays in motion once it is set in motion—until another object, such as this egg, affects it.

Content consultant: Kevin Finerghty, Adjunct Professor of Geology, State University of New York at Oswego

Lerner Publications Company
A division of Lerner Publishing Group, Inc.
241 First Avenue North
Minneapolis, MN 55401 USA

For reading levels and more information, look up this title at www.lernerbooks.com.

Main body text set in Diverda Serif Com. Typeface provided by Linotype AG.

Library of Congress Cataloging-in-Publication Data

Marsico, Katie, 1980– author.
    Key discoveries in physical science / by Katie Marsico.
        pages   cm — (Science discovery timelines)
    Includes bibliographical references and index.
    Summary: "Explore this fascinating timeline history of physical science! What are matter, motion, gravity, electricity, magnetism, and substances? Who first studied these concepts? And who later built on and expanded the work of those early thinkers?"— Provided by publisher.
    ISBN 978-1-4677-5785-0 (lib. bdg. : alk. paper)
    ISBN 978-1-4677-6251-9 (eBook)
    1. Physical sciences—History—Juvenile literature. 2. Matter—History—Juvenile literature. 3. Chemistry—History—Juvenile literature. 4. Motion—History—Juvenile literature. 5. Force and energy—History—Juvenile literature. I. Title.
Q163.M364 2015
500.209—dc23   2014016208

Manufactured in the United States of America
1 — BP — 12/31/14

CONTENTS

INTRODUCTION

Physical science is the branch of science that deals with nonliving materials and how they work. It is also an amazing story shaped by people's efforts to understand the world around them. In ancient times, the topics of matter, chemical reactions, motion, forces, and energy were confusing and mysterious. The scientific process of forming a hypothesis, or educated prediction, and testing it with experiments wasn't common practice.

Instead, ancient philosophers, or scholars, relied on their personal beliefs and observations, as well as what knowledge of the universe was available to them. They made statements about physical science that weren't always right. Still, for thousands of years, the world accepted most of their explanations. The opinions of those philosophers also became important stepping-stones that the first physical scientists based further exploration upon. So did the work of alchemists, who conducted experiments in the hopes of changing less valuable metals into gold or finding ways to lengthen a person's life. Yet their ideas tended to be clouded by the mystical nature of alchemy itself.

Ultimately, people figured out more controlled methods of collecting data. They used math and science laws to explain everything from the tiniest pieces of matter to the entire universe. Along the way, they answered questions about topics ranging from the air they breathed to the speed of falling objects. These scientists harnessed the power of chemical reactions, magnetism, and electricity. Their theories and inventions forever changed the face of physics and chemistry.

The stories of physical science and how it developed can be told through a series of timelines. Each one shows how philosophers, mathematicians, and scientists were linked in their quest for knowledge. It wasn't unusual for them to argue, compete, and disprove one another's ideas. Yet some also worked together in the same laboratories as they searched for answers about the world around them. Either way, they became characters joined by remarkable milestones. Their struggles, successes, and discoveries are all entries on the far-reaching timelines of physical science.

This ancient Egyptian painting from the twelfth century BCE tells the story of the sun's journey through the heavens and back again. Ancient philosophers explained the world around them by guessing based on their observations.

A Line That Shows a Story

A timeline is a visual representation of history. It displays a series of events and the dates on which they happened. These entries are related to a common theme or period of time and are listed chronologically. That means they are arranged in the order in which they occurred.

Timelines tell a story by placing key moments in a logical sequence. They also help people understand the cause-and-effect relationship among events. In some cases, timelines span hundreds of thousands of years. In others, they only stretch across a period of minutes. Artwork often accompanies the entries in a timeline. Finally, dates that occurred before a certain point in history (in Christian tradition, the birth of Jesus Christ) frequently include the abbreviation *BCE*, which stands for "Before the Common Era."

Each chapter in this book begins with a timeline and then moves to a written story. You can read the chapters in the way that helps you understand the content best. Look at the visual highlights first and then read the details. Or start by reading the text and then go back to the timelines to view the order in which key events happened.

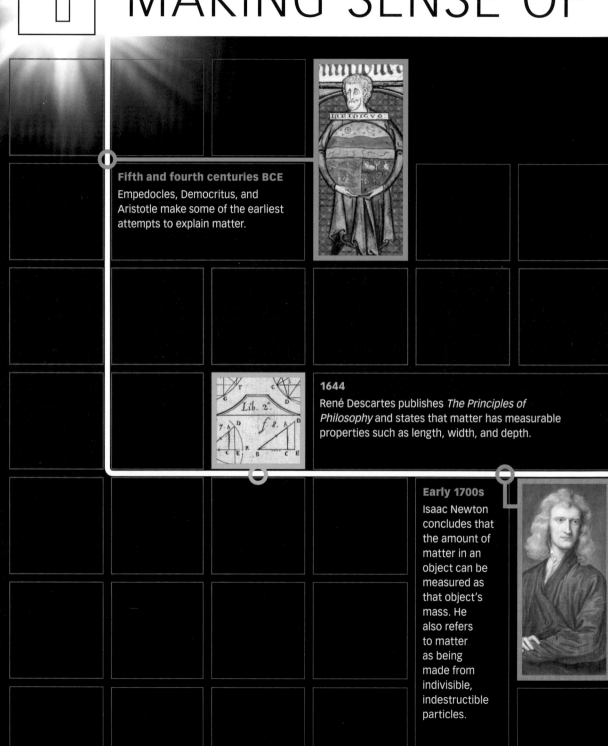

Fifth and fourth centuries BCE

Empedocles, Democritus, and Aristotle make some of the earliest attempts to explain matter.

1644

René Descartes publishes *The Principles of Philosophy* and states that matter has measurable properties such as length, width, and depth.

Early 1700s

Isaac Newton concludes that the amount of matter in an object can be measured as that object's mass. He also refers to matter as being made from indivisible, indestructible particles.

MATTER

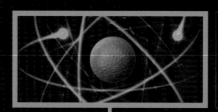

1904

J. J. Thomson uses his discovery of electrons to suggest that an atom's structure resembles plum pudding.

1911

Ernest Rutherford uses his discovery of protons in an atom's nucleus to suggest that atomic structure more closely resembles the solar system.

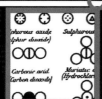

1803

John Dalton reveals his atomic theory, which states that all matter is made from basic

Ancient Greek philosophers were some of the first people who tried to explain matter—the materials and substances that form all physical objects. What made up Earth and everything in it? What were the most basic building blocks of the world? Empedocles, Democritus, and Aristotle attempted to answer such questions. These men were scholars and teachers who were highly respected for their knowledge. Aristotle even tutored famous Macedonian king and conqueror Alexander the Great. The philosophers' social influence was why people so often simply accepted their ideas as true.

In about 450 BCE, Empedocles declared that the universe was made up of four main elements: earth, water, fire, and air. (Sometimes written records aren't always clear about precisely when ancient philosophers formed their opinions. As a result, historians often have to rely on estimated dates.) Not long afterward, Democritus studied how these elements mixed together. He paid attention to how mud was formed by adding earth, or soil, to water. He recognized that once blended, the two elements were not easily separated.

The figure in this image holds the four elements of the universe: earth, water, fire, and air.

Democritus believed that nothing could come from nothing. So he reasoned that tiny particles were the smallest building blocks of physical objects. According to Democritus, these particles joined together in different combinations and patterns to form different physical materials. He described them using the term *atomos*, which is Greek for "indivisible." Democritus chose this word because he thought the particles could neither be destroyed nor divided into smaller pieces.

Microscopes hadn't been invented yet, so Democritus couldn't get a close-up view of atoms. Yet he believed they were constantly in motion and had physical features that allowed them to cling together. These features included hooks, sockets, and eyes!

More than one hundred years after Democritus expressed his views on matter, Aristotle publicly challenged them. During the fourth century BCE, he noted that Democritus said atoms moved but didn't say *why*. Aristotle found that unacceptable. He believed there had to be a reason that everything in the world was the way it was.

He supported Empedocles's description of Earth's basic physical materials. Aristotle also began using the term *hulē* to talk about matter. This is the Greek word for "wood." Aristotle said that like wood, matter was a raw material that took different forms after being involved in physical changes and processes. He described hulē as having properties such as hot, cold, moist, and dry.

WHOSE IDEA **WAS IT?**

Democritus was the student of another Greek philosopher—Leucippus *(right)*. Some people, including Aristotle, believed it was Leucippus who came up with the idea of atoms. They said Democritus simply described his teacher's thoughts in greater detail. Democritus was also more well known than Leucippus. This may be why he received more credit for early theories about atoms. Either way, it's likely both men worked together to develop their ideas about matter and the universe.

The tale of Democritus and Leucippus isn't unique in the larger story of physical science. Debate about who first discovered something stretches as far back as ancient Greece. Sometimes, it stems from rivalry between men and women of science. Often, however, it happens because scientists work together as a team or conduct similar experiments at roughly the same time. Then it can be difficult to tell who deserves more credit. What has always been clear is that scientists depend and build upon one another's knowledge.

Such ideas remained more popular than those of Democritus for several centuries. Aristotle's connections to powerful figures such as Alexander the Great added to public awe of his wisdom. As a result, most people didn't question or try to improve his way of thinking. During the 1600s, however, René Descartes finally cracked the long-standing beliefs Aristotle and the scientific community had developed.

A MORE MECHANICAL **VIEW OF MATTER**

Descartes was a French mathematician. He was also a philosopher, like Aristotle. Descartes lived in seventeenth-century Europe and devoted much of his time to the study of geometry. As a philosopher, he reflected upon what matter truly was. As a mathematician, he became convinced that geometry could help explain it.

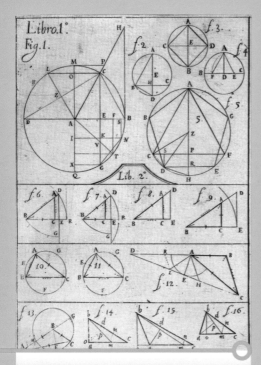

Descartes used concepts from seventeenth-century geometry to explain the properties of matter.

In 1644 Descartes declared that matter had measurable properties such as length, width, and depth. He discussed his ideas in a book called *The Principles of Philosophy*. Afterward, Descartes's use of geometry became an important stepping-stone. His work bridged a gap between ancient philosophers and later scientists searching for a more mechanical understanding of matter.

In the early 1700s, British physicist and mathematician Isaac Newton continued to build upon Descartes's ideas. Newton declared that the amount of matter that made up an object could be measured as that object's mass. He also explained matter using a description that had been rejected more than two thousand years earlier. Newton said it was built out of "solid, massy, hard, impenetrable, movable particles [that were] . . . even so very hard as never to wear or break in pieces."

REVISITING THE **IDEA OF ATOMS**

The notion of indestructible, indivisible particles had been suggested once before—by Democritus in ancient Greece! In 1803 English scientist John Dalton reviewed Democritus's work, as well as more recent ideas about matter. Since Dalton had always been fascinated by air, weather, and the atmosphere, he was experimenting with gases. That's when he noticed that water absorbed carbon dioxide more easily than it took in nitrogen. Why was this happening?

Dalton concluded that it must have something to do with how each substance was formed. Thanks to Descartes and Newton, Dalton realized that all matter could be described using qualities such as mass. Of course, different substances still had different properties. Thanks to Democritus, Dalton suspected that these unique qualities existed in an element's tiniest pieces, or particles. Dalton reasoned that this would cause the particles of different elements to react differently with one another.

In 1803 Dalton breathed new life into Democritus's ideas when Dalton revealed his atomic theory. He said his experiments proved that at its most basic level, all matter was made up of atoms. Every element was formed by atoms unique to that element. In turn, atoms of different chemical elements joined together to form more complicated substances, or compounds. Like Democritus, Dalton believed that atoms could be neither destroyed nor divided.

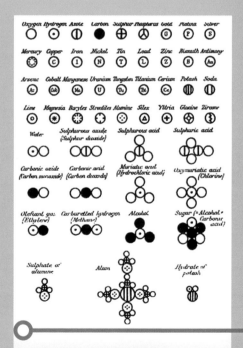

John Dalton drew symbols to represent the atoms of basic elements, as shown in the top rows of this chart. The symbols in the bottom rows represent compounds.

UNDERSTANDING **ATOMIC STRUCTURE**

Dalton used wooden spheres to craft early models of the atom. In 1904 English physicist J. J. Thomson developed another visual aid, as well as a theory about the structure of atoms. Thomson had been working with a brand-new invention called the cathode-ray tube. This device was made up of glowing rays of light that followed electrical flow within a vacuum tube. Many years later, this invention was used in television sets. Scientists were eager to learn more about the rays that passed between the cathodes, or conductors, on either end of the tube.

Thomson noticed that the cathodes caused the light rays to change direction. He predicted that this happened because tiny particles in the rays carried a negative electrical charge. Such charges are a property of matter. They can be either positive or negative. Similar charges repel each other, and opposite charges attract each other. Reactions between charges allow matter to experience different forces.

As Thomson experimented with the cathode-ray tube, he determined that the negatively charged particles he observed had far less mass than any atom. This meant that atoms could indeed be divided into smaller pieces. They *weren't* the tiniest building blocks of matter!

Thomson had discovered electrons, or negatively charged subatomic particles. This knowledge completely changed how the world viewed atoms. To help people visualize atomic structure, Thomson compared it to plum pudding—a rich holiday pudding filled with either plums or raisins. He said the "plums" were particles that carried a negative charge. The "pudding" was the positively charged matter surrounding them.

In 1911 British physicist Ernest Rutherford took Thomson's model a step further. He had just finished several experiments with radiation. That's energy released in the form of waves or subatomic particles. One of Rutherford's most famous experiments involved firing radioactive particles through thin gold foil. He observed that most of the particles—which carried a positive charge—passed through the foil. Yet an extremely small number of them bounced off the gold.

Rutherford knew that particles with opposite charges attract each other. He also knew that particles with similar charges repel each other. So he realized that Thomson's model of the atom wasn't totally correct. If the gold atoms were mainly filled with positive matter, or pudding, more

of the particles fired at the gold foil should have bounced back.

Rutherford's experiment made him think that atomic structure was more like the solar system than like plum pudding. He believed that most of an atom's mass was located in a small, dense center, which scientists later called a nucleus. This part of the atom held positively charged particles, or protons. Rutherford compared the nucleus to the sun and said that it was mainly surrounded by empty space. He added that negatively charged electrons moved in circular patterns around the nucleus. Rutherford likened their motion to planets orbiting the sun.

Yet it wasn't long before scientists, including Rutherford himself, started questioning this atomic model. Thanks to Rutherford's work, they knew that each element was made up of atoms that held a unique number of protons. Physicists used that number of protons to assign every element an atomic number. Scientists had also figured out that an element's atomic number was equal to roughly half its atomic mass.

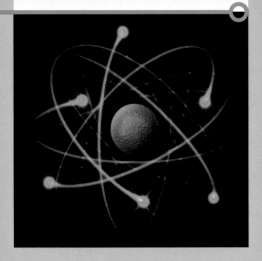

Ernest Rutherford suggested that atomic structure was like the solar system, with a nucleus representing the sun and electrons orbiting the nucleus like planets.

If these facts were correct, however, something didn't add up. Rutherford's colleague, British physicist James Chadwick, also wanted to know what—besides protons—was in the nucleus that added to an atom's mass. Rutherford suspected atoms contained a third piece that had neither a negative nor a positive charge.

In 1932 Chadwick uncovered proof of this neutral piece. His experiment involved using radiation to bombard—or fire a stream of high-energy particles against—nitrogen atoms. Chadwick then trapped the atoms in a chamber where they reacted with gas to create electrical charges. By studying how these charges flowed, he was able to determine the mass and speed of both the atoms and their subatomic particles. This revealed the presence of something besides protons and electrons. By bombarding atoms, Chadwick had forced the nucleus to release large, neutral particles called neutrons.

FUTURE MILESTONES
INVOLVING MATTER

Of course, Chadwick's work wasn't the end of the story. Eventually, scientists discovered additional subatomic particles—quarks and leptons! Continuing to identify tinier and tinier building blocks of matter has helped people understand more about both everyday objects and the universe they exist in. For example, such efforts have allowed scientists to learn more about what creates and affects the various forces that act on matter. In the future, it's possible people will find even smaller subatomic particles. In turn, these milestones would likely reveal even more information about how atoms react to one another.

Nuclear energy, or the energy released when an atom's nucleus splits, is the result of one such reaction. The work of Rutherford and Chadwick laid the foundation for scientists who would go on to explore nuclear energy and its uses. In the 1940s, researchers learned that nuclear power could fuel deadly weapons. In 1945, during World War II (1939–1945), the United States dropped atomic bombs on two Japanese cities, Hiroshima and Nagasaki, causing widespread death and destruction.

When an atom's nucleus splits, the fragments shoot out sideways. This process is called fission, and it's a big part of how nuclear energy is produced.

Yet nuclear power doesn't necessarily have to cause tragedy. By 2002 scientists had figured out how nuclear energy could create 16 percent of the world's electricity. More than a decade later, they are still investigating how to safely harness nuclear power to provide people with heat and light. If these scientists succeed, they might be able to reduce pollution by allowing us to depend less on energy sources such as coal and gas. Future milestones in the story of matter will likely reflect their achievements, as well as their ability to use any new knowledge about atoms and matter responsibly.

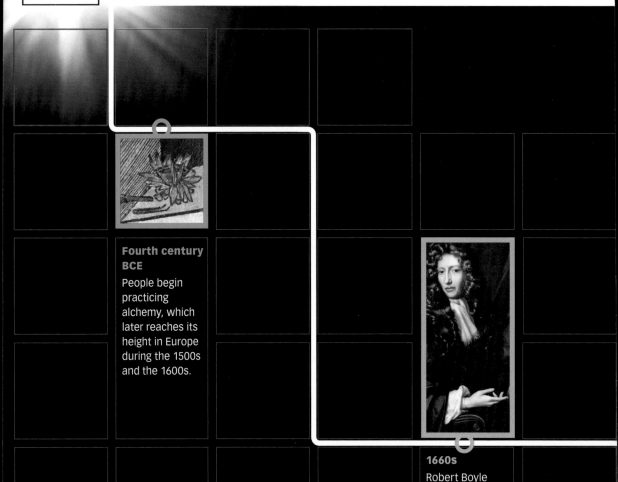

Fourth century BCE

People begin practicing alchemy, which later reaches its height in Europe during the 1500s and the 1600s.

1660s

Robert Boyle concludes that Earth's simplest

1869

Dmitri Mendeleev relies on atomic weight to create the periodic table of elements. He proves that studying gaps in the table can help predict the properties of undiscovered elements.

1913

Henry Moseley uses each element's atomic number to reorganize the periodic table.

1789

Antoine-Laurent Lavoisier publishes the first modern chemistry textbook, which describes the process he used to name and organize thirty-three separate elements.

1898

Marie Sklodowska Curie and Pierre Curie announce their discovery of the radioactive elements radium and polonium. They spend the next several years researching these substances to prove how they fit into the periodic table.

Explaining matter is only one chapter in the story of physical science. Another chapter—chemistry—took shape when people began exploring the structure and properties of everyday substances. People wanted to understand reactions between different types of matter, as well as how matter changed forms. At first, such curiosity was mainly fueled by people's awe of precious metals. As far back as 4600 BCE, cultures around the globe have viewed gold as a treasure and a sign of great wealth. Many saw it as one of the purest forms of matter. Alchemists even searched for ways to transform less valuable metals into gold. This pursuit dates back to the fourth century BCE. It reached its height in Europe during the 1500s and the 1600s. Alchemists also tried to create potions that would cure illness, ease pain, and lengthen a person's life.

Before people more fully understood matter, many of the substances alchemists mixed and heated in cauldrons remained a mystery. Alchemy,

Gold *(above)* is a metal that has been valued by cultures across the globe for centuries. An alchemist *(right)* experiments with heating and mixing substances to make gold.

however, set the stage for the experiments and discoveries that later shaped chemistry. Alchemists studied the different properties of matter. Alchemists also tested how substances reacted with one another and took new forms.

A MORE **SCIENTIFIC APPROACH**

People were in awe of alchemy, but they were also suspicious of it. Alchemists sometimes used strange, secret symbols when writing about their work. They also offered mystical explanations for changes in matter. Still, alchemists' curiosity about chemical reactions became a jumping-off point for scientists to practice chemistry. In fact, some of the world's earliest chemists were quite familiar with alchemy!

One early chemist was Irish scientist and philosopher Robert Boyle. His experiments in the 1660s helped bridge the gap between alchemy and chemistry. During Boyle's life, the world still accepted ancient philosophers' ideas about matter. It took courage to question what had already been explained by men such as Aristotle.

Yet Boyle did far more than question ancient theories about matter. He conducted controlled tests to see if they were right. Boyle also recorded how he carried out these tests and what they showed. He used a scientific process to help people understand what they had once viewed as mystical reactions.

One of Boyle's best-known experiments involved pumping air into a glass container. He observed how the air—which he knew was a gas—shrunk to fit inside a closed space. In other words, its volume decreased. Boyle also noticed that when gas was trapped, the pressure it put on the container's walls increased. He realized that gas could behave this way only if it was formed by tiny particles.

Boyle's experiments showed something else too. He used a current, or stream, of electricity to break down water into two different gases. Yet the gases themselves couldn't be broken down any further. So Boyle reasoned that the gases had to be elements—Earth's simplest substances. This theory led people to rethink Aristotle's ideas about earth, fire, water, and air. Scientists started to view elements as matter made from tiny particles that couldn't be reduced to a purer form.

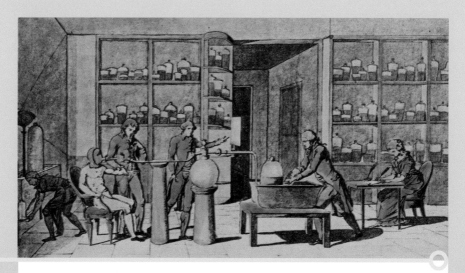

Marie Lavoisier made this engraving of her husband, Antoine Lavoisier, experimenting with chemical reactions in the eighteenth century.

IDENTIFYING THE **ELEMENTS**

Later, scientists explored questions Boyle hadn't been able to answer. For example, he didn't know the identities of all the elements or how many existed. French scientist Antoine-Laurent Lavoisier tried to solve these mysteries in the late 1700s.

Lavoisier had been hired by the French government to improve the way gunpowder was produced. This meant he worked in what was, at that time, an impressive lab. Lavoisier could carry out detailed experiments. He watched what happened when different substances were mixed together or heated. He also became one of the first scientists to describe chemical reactions using quantitative data.

Lavoisier took precise measurements of mass with a balance scale that he had designed. He learned that the mass of any substance before a reaction equaled the mass of any substance after a reaction. That meant matter was neither created nor destroyed during a chemical reaction. This scientific fact became known as the law of conservation of mass.

Measuring mass also helped Lavoisier figure out that both air and water were made from separate elements. He named these substances carbon, hydrogen, and oxygen. They were among a list of thirty-three elements described by Lavoisier. He organized the elements into four groups—gases, metals, nonmetals, and earth. Lavoisier chose names for them by using Greek or Latin root words that hinted at each element's properties.

In 1789 Lavoisier published a book discussing his ideas about elements, compounds, and chemical reactions. Later, many people said it was the first modern chemistry textbook. Of course, future scientists continued to make important discoveries. In the 1800s, new knowledge about atoms and their weights changed the face of chemistry.

PART OF A PATTERN

When Russian chemist Dmitri Mendeleev taught chemistry in the late 1860s, he realized that he needed an updated textbook. Mendeleev decided to write it himself. What he ended up creating, however, reached far beyond his own classroom. At that point, scientists had identified more than sixty elements, as well as their atomic masses, or weights.

In 1869 Mendeleev organized all the known elements in horizontal

A WIFE'S WORK IN THE LAB

Women were rarely acknowledged as scientists in eighteenth-century France. And they didn't have the same opportunities as men. Yet that didn't stop women from helping to achieve scientific milestones. Lavoisier's wife, Marie, spent the early years of her marriage studying chemistry. She also learned English, which allowed her to read about the work of British scientists. Marie became a skilled artist too. She used her talent to sketch and engrave images of the tools in Lavoisier's lab. Experts believe Marie also helped her husband record data from his experiments. Even after Lavoisier's death in 1794, Marie continued to host scientific discussions at her home.

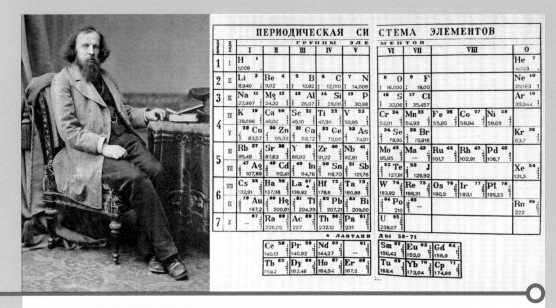

ПЕРИОДИЧЕСКАЯ СИСТЕМА ЭЛЕМЕНТОВ

In 1868 Dmitri Mendeleev *(left)* arranged all the known elements in order of increasing atomic weight. His periodic table of elements *(right)* helped scientists predict chemistry discoveries that lay ahead.

rows. He arranged them in order of increasing atomic weight. That's when Mendeleev started to see a pattern. For the most part, elements with similar chemical properties ended up in the same vertical columns. Highly reactive metals such as lithium and sodium, for instance, fell into the same group. So did reactive nonmetals such as chlorine and bromine. Yet Mendeleev noticed that he could rely on atomic weight to create these patterns only if he left certain spots on his chart blank. He suspected that the blanks would one day be filled by undiscovered elements. Mendeleev believed he could even predict what properties these substances would have from studying patterns in the chart. When scientists identified gallium, scandium, and germanium between 1875 and 1886, he was proven right!

Mendeleev's periodic table of elements offered a glimpse into the future of chemistry. The world suddenly had a rough idea of what discoveries lay ahead. Yet the table also presented a greater challenge to other scientists, including Marie Sklodowska Curie and Pierre Curie.

THE RISKS OF
EXPLORING RADIATION

Milestones in physical science often involve people exploring the unknown. But sometimes such explorers pay a heavy price. This was true for Marie Curie. In the late 1800s and the early 1900s, the world was unaware of all the health risks linked to radioactive substances. Regular contact with radiation left Curie exhausted and ill. It cracked and burned her skin. In 1934 Curie died of leukemia. Experts believe her death was caused by a lifetime of working with radioactive elements. Thanks to Curie, people don't just understand radiation better. They also grasp how dangerous it can be and why it must be handled with care.

In 1898 the wife-and-husband team announced they had discovered two new elements in the mineral pitchblende. The Curies named them polonium and radium and said they were highly radioactive. That meant the elements released large amounts of radiation.

At the time, radiation was at the heart of exciting scientific breakthroughs such as X-ray machines. Yet that didn't guarantee polonium and radium spots on the periodic table. First, the Curies had to prove how their elements fit into the patterns Mendeleev had seen. This meant figuring out their atomic weights and chemical properties.

The Curies faced a huge scientific challenge. For starters, they'd have to isolate, or separate, atoms of both

Marie *(seated)* and Pierre Curie discovered and studied the radioactive elements polonium and radium, eventually proving to other scientists that these elements belonged on the periodic table.

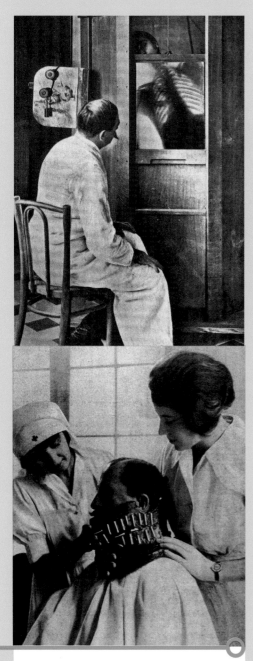

In the early 1900s, radiation was at the heart of exciting scientific breakthroughs such as X-ray machines *(above)* and early cancer treatments *(below)*.

elements from the pitchblende. Sometimes only traces of polonium and radium were found in an entire mound of this mineral. It was also difficult to observe the elements' chemical properties. The Curies found it far easier to study the radiation in these elements. For these reasons, some scientists weren't sure radioactive substances should be added to the periodic table.

The Curies spent years exploring radium and polonium. They were able to isolate the first but not the second. Yet they still gathered enough data about each element to convince scientists that both existed. Thanks to the Curies' efforts, the world also learned more about radiation. By 1905 both radium and polonium appeared in the periodic table of elements.

In 1913 British physicist Henry Moseley reordered Mendeleev's chart. More elements had been added since the 1860s, and not all of them fit properly. Moseley guessed that the periodic table relied too heavily on atomic weight. In some cases, this arrangement was forcing elements with different properties into the same column. A few years earlier, Ernest Rutherford had learned that atoms contain protons. Moseley believed that the number of protons in an atom had a greater effect on the element's chemical properties than atomic weight did.

Using X-rays, he counted how many protons were present in each element. He then worked with these numbers—the atomic numbers of the elements—to rebuild the periodic table. Moseley arranged the elements in order of increasing atomic number. Suddenly, pieces of the puzzle that hadn't fit before snapped into place! Moseley's discovery pushed elements with similar properties into the right groups.

ACHIEVING **LIFE-CHANGING ADVANCES**

People have made other changes to the periodic table since 1913. The most recent element to be added to the table was discovered in 2013. Scientists are still working on an official name for it. At that point, there were 118 elements in the table. No one knows how many more will be added in the future.

Scientists also continue to explore the chemical properties of existing elements. They have already found several ways to put these substances to practical use. Starting in the early 1900s, doctors began treating cancer with radium. Pierre Curie was the earliest scientist to suggest that radium could help combat this often deadly disease. In 1901 he experimented with radium salts wrapped in rubber coating. Curie noticed that when he placed the salts on his arm, they burned his flesh. By studying his wound, he eventually concluded that radium was capable of injuring or even killing living cells.

Medical researchers built on the Curies' work and started using radium to target cancer cells. Scientists still conduct experiments with this element in the hopes of creating even more aggressive cancer treatments. The growing understanding of substances such as radium will undoubtedly lead to life-changing milestones and other exciting chapters in the story of physical science.

Fourth century BCE

Aristotle explains movement in terms of forced and natural motion. He also declares that Earth and the heavens are controlled by different laws of motion.

1589–1592

Galileo conducts experiments that challenge Aristotle's idea about how weight affects the motion of falling objects.

1604

Galileo begins studying the movement of bronze balls along inclined planes, which he eventually uses to demonstrate uniform acceleration.

MOTION

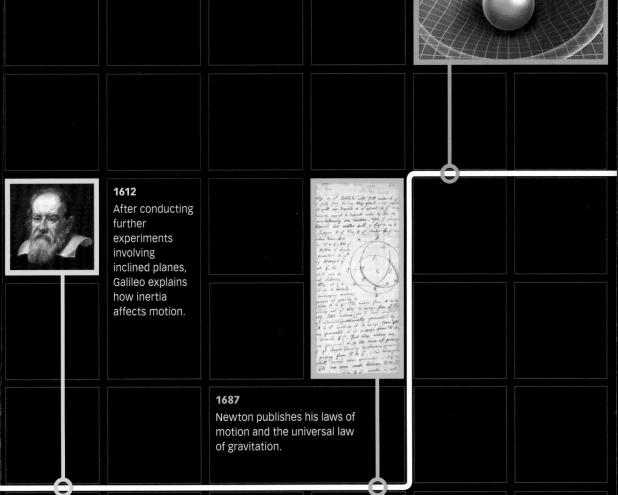

1915
Albert Einstein reveals his general theory of relativity, which revises some of Newton's ideas by exploring gravity's relationship with inertia, as well as its relationship with space and time.

1612
After conducting further experiments involving inclined planes, Galileo explains how inertia affects motion.

1687
Newton publishes his laws of motion and the universal law of gravitation.

Even the earliest human beings understood that matter moved. What was less clear was how and why it moved. People wondered what forces set both everyday objects and entire planets in motion. Their search for answers led to many important milestones in physics.

Aristotle focused on more than basic materials. During the fourth century BCE, he also tried to explain motion. Like Empedocles, he believed that Earth was made of four main elements—earth, water, air, and fire. Aristotle reasoned that natural forces of attraction and repulsion existed between each of them. So a stone tossed in the air returned to the ground because both objects were forms of earth. They were therefore drawn to each other. At the same time, the stone and the sky above the ground repelled each other. He figured this happened because they were composed of different elements—earth and air.

Aristotle suggested that such movement was natural motion. He also argued that the speed of a falling object was affected by the weight of the object. Based on his ideas, if a 40-pound (18-kilogram) stone was dropped from a cliff, it would fall twice as fast as a 20-pound (9.1 kg) stone.

Aristotle believed in forced, or violent, motion as well. This type of motion featured someone or something putting an outside force on an object. A person throwing a stone into the air would have been an example of violent motion. This action was caused by an outside trigger instead of by attraction or repulsion among the four main elements. Once the forces behind violent motion stopped acting on an object, he believed, the object would stop moving. So a stone tossed toward the sky wouldn't keep traveling upward forever. Eventually, it would fall.

Finally, Aristotle said Earth and the heavens were controlled by different rules of motion. According to his logic, a "Prime Mover" affected the movement of the stars and planets. Aristotle sometimes referred to the Prime Mover as "God." He didn't worship this being or encourage people to view it with religious awe. Instead, Aristotle—who was convinced that everything in the universe existed for a specific reason—thought of the Prime Mover as a necessary presence. The idea of such a being explained why the star-filled heavens were the way they were.

UPDATING **ARISTOTLE'S IDEAS**

People relied upon Aristotle's beliefs about motion for many centuries. Yet it's doubtful he ever tested his opinions by collecting precise data about moving objects. Galileo Galilei was an Italian astronomer and physicist. During the late 1500s and the early 1600s, he became famous for questioning several of Aristotle's thoughts on motion.

Unlike Aristotle, Galileo carried out careful and often controlled experiments. He conducted a test involving an iron ball weighing 1 pound (0.45 kg) and another weighing 10 pounds (4.5 kg). He dropped both from the same height at the same moment. Galileo observed how they hit the ground at roughly the same time. He was convinced he had disproved Aristotle's ideas about weight and speed. But Galileo wanted to understand and explain *why* he got the results he did. So next, he focused on how the speed of a falling object changes as it moves downward.

Galileo knew that to make accurate observations about speed, he'd need to somehow slow down whatever motion he was trying to observe. In 1604 Galileo studied the motion of different-sized bronze balls rolling down a ramp. Every second, Galileo noted how far each one traveled.

He discovered that weight didn't impact how the balls accelerated. Their speed increased at a uniform rate—especially if they didn't encounter much resistance. It was this resistance and Aristotle's ideas about violent motion that Galileo investigated next. According to Aristotle, once an outside force stopped acting on an object, that object would stop moving. Yet, if this was true, why did an arrow shot from a bow keep flying until it hit something? Why didn't it just fall to the ground?

This painting shows Galileo dropping iron balls from Italy's Leaning Tower of Pisa. Historians debate the details of Galileo's experiment, but they generally agree that the scientist didn't actually drop anything from this famous building.

CHALLENGING
THE CHURCH

Disagreeing with Aristotle's theories was risky. It involved taking a stand against popular ideas that had been in place for many generations. This often upset powerful people, including Pope Urban VIII. The pope headed the Roman Catholic Church, which was a major influence in Europe when Galileo lived. Some Catholics were especially bothered by Galileo's statements about the heavens.

In 1609 Galileo built his own telescope and used it to study the solar system. What he saw helped him learn about the motion of the sun and planets. Galileo *(below, center)* realized that Earth moved around the sun. Aristotle had suggested just the opposite. His view was closer to the Catholics' belief that God had placed Earth at the center of the universe. Galileo paid a price for daring to challenge these ideas. The pope banned one of his books. Galileo was also put under house arrest from 1633 until his death in 1642.

In 1612 Galileo said it was because objects set into motion would stay in motion unless they met with resistance. To demonstrate this property of matter, called inertia, he placed two wooden inclined planes across from each other. When he rolled a marble downward from any height on the first plane, it traveled upward toward the same height on the second plane.

When Galileo made the wood smoother by sanding it, the marble moved even farther along the second plane. He said this was because the smoother wood created less friction, or resistance, between the surfaces of the plane and the marble. If friction didn't exist, he suspected that the marble would have stayed in motion. Ultimately, Galileo believed, the marble would have rolled all the way to its original height on the second plane.

FROM APPLES
TO EARTH ITSELF

Galileo's understanding of movement was reflected in the work of Isaac Newton several decades later. In 1687 Newton published his laws of motion and universal law of gravitation. According to one popular story, he was inspired to create the laws after being hit on the head by an apple that fell off a tree. Supposedly, this made him wonder about the motion of the falling fruit. Newton questioned why the apple fell and what affected its speed as it dropped to the ground.

Centuries later, no one can be certain if this account is indeed true. What is clear is that Newton was deeply fascinated with both motion and astronomy. As he admired the night sky through a telescope, he asked himself what forces kept the stars and planets from falling out of the heavens.

Newton spent several years studying both astronomy and the motion of many different falling objects. He also exchanged letters filled with discussions and debates about the universe with other scientists and mathematicians. Along the way, he developed and relied upon calculus. This branch of math allowed Newton to explain and test his ideas about motion using mathematical laws.

Newton's first law of motion restated Galileo's theory that an object in motion tended to stay in motion and that an object at rest tended to stay at rest. Changes to how an object moved or rested were caused by outside forces.

The second law of motion said that how an object moved was a direct result of the forces acting on it. Here Newton used a mathematical equation to help people understand exactly what force was. He said that force (F) was equal to an object's mass (M) multiplied by the rate at which it accelerated (A). So, $F = MA$.

His third law of motion stated that for any action there was an equal and opposite reaction. When one object pushed another object, it got pushed back with the same level of force. In addition to his laws of motion, Newton formed a theory about gravity that changed the way people viewed the universe. He said gravity was a force that attracted objects to the center of Earth. It explained why apples—or any objects—naturally moved toward the ground.

Yet Newton also believed that forces of gravity existed between *all* the planets. Newton rejected Aristotle's idea that there were different laws of motion for Earth and the heavens. As Newton explained, it was gravity that kept the sun, the moon, stars, and planets from crashing downward.

In addition, Newton said that both mass and distance affected gravitational force. The greater the mass of two objects, the greater the force of gravity between them. The greater the distance between two objects, the weaker the force of gravity between them.

Newton's laws retooled the way people understood both motion and the universe. In later years, famous scientists such as German physicist Albert Einstein further built upon them. Thanks to Newton, Einstein was able to develop his own important physics theories in the early 1900s. He made changes to Newton's laws that allowed him to better explain the speed of light, as well as how time and space are connected to motion.

EINSTEIN'S IDEAS ON **GRAVITY**

In 1915 Einstein unveiled his general theory of relativity. This theory reshaped Newton's ideas about gravity. Einstein said that from a moving object, it was impossible to tell the difference between gravity and inertia. Someone inside a spinning spacecraft, for example, would move toward the craft's outer walls. This motion might feel like the effect of gravity. Yet it would actually be due to inertia. Of course, it would be hard for a spinning person to tell gravity apart from inertia because he or she would already be moving.

Einstein also explained that gravity wasn't so much a force as a reaction to a curve in space and time. The curve was what triggered objects to move. This idea is often explained by describing how a bowling ball causes the surface of a trampoline to stretch and dip. A marble placed close to the bowling ball rolls toward the dip. In Einstein's mind, a star, a planet, or another extremely large object was like the bowling ball. It had enough mass to create a curve in space and time or, in this case, the trampoline. A meteorite or any smaller object was like the marble. It moved because it was pulled toward the curve formed by the larger object.

Scientists continue to test the limits of Newton's laws of motion. No one knows exactly what they will learn, but new discoveries may someday change how spacecraft are launched into orbit.

TESTING THE **LIMITS OF MOTION**

Modern scientists continue to explore motion and forces. The work of Newton and other early physicists is used in everything from automobile production to space exploration. People are always searching for new ways to travel farther and move faster. As a result, they continue to test the limits of motion. Researchers in Germany recently carried out experiments that may challenge Newton's third law of motion.

In 2013 these scientists observed the movement of lasers in two loops of fiber-optic cable. Fiber-optic technology relies upon thin threads of glass or plastic to transmit information in the form of light signals. Physicists watched how opposite pulses of light reacted with each other in the fiber-optic loops. The interaction between the pulses caused them to accelerate in the same direction. Scientists also noticed that this acceleration resulted in no equal and opposite push-back movement.

These physicists are still in the early stages of research. Yet what they learn could spark technology that allows for faster, more efficient communication. It could even alter the way rockets and other spacecraft are launched into orbit! Such suggestions might seem fantastic now. One day, however, they may become remarkable milestones in the timelines of physical science.

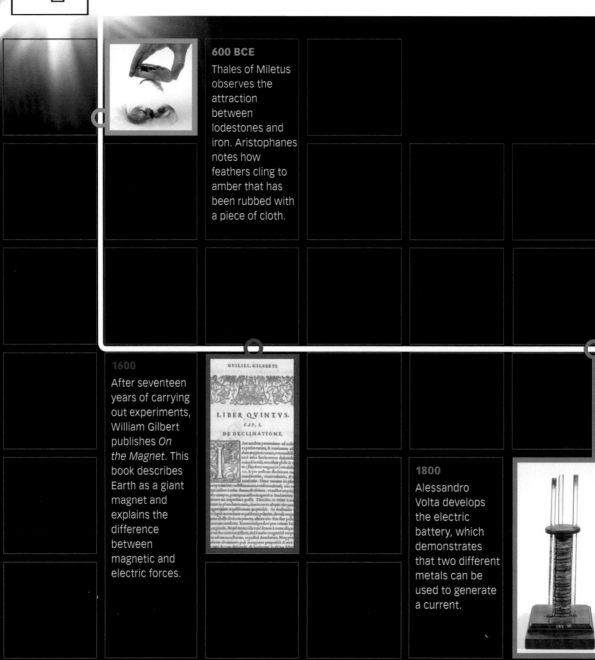

600 BCE
Thales of Miletus observes the attraction between lodestones and iron. Aristophanes notes how feathers cling to amber that has been rubbed with a piece of cloth.

1600
After seventeen years of carrying out experiments, William Gilbert publishes *On the Magnet*. This book describes Earth as a giant magnet and explains the difference between magnetic and electric forces.

GVILIEL. GILBERTI

LIBER QVINTVS.
CAP. I.
DE DECLINATIONE.

1800
Alessandro Volta develops the electric battery, which demonstrates that two different metals can be used to generate a current.

FORCES

1831
Michael Faraday discovers electromagnetic induction.

1882
Thomas Edison relies upon electromagnetic generators to produce direct current (DC) electricity, which is then used to light 193 buildings in New York City.

1820
While conducting two unrelated experiments, Hans Christian Ørsted notices the way an electric current causes a magnetic needle to move. Later that year, André-Marie Ampère proves that the direction of currents in parallel wires creates different magnetic forces.

1884
Nikola Tesla unsuccessfully tries to persuade Edison to use the forces formed by a rotating magnetic field to create and distribute alternating current (AC) electricity.

The story of physical science isn't limited to a list of laws and equations. By studying electromagnetism, scientists figured out new ways to create and use energy. What they learned helped them power motors and light city streets. Before that happened, however, people spent several centuries simply trying to understand magnetism and electricity.

Even in ancient times, it was obvious that some minerals possessed amazing powers of attraction. In 600 BCE, the Greek philosopher Thales of Miletus recorded that iron was drawn to lodestones found near the city of Magnesia. He tried to understand how these rocks, which would later be identified as the mineral magnetite, were able to attract iron. Thales supposed it was because they had a spirit, or a soul. Eventually, people started to refer to the magical rocks as "magnets."

Another Greek philosopher, Aristophanes, noticed amber also had powers of attraction. He observed that rubbing the mineral with a piece of fur caused feathers to stick to it. Aristophanes believed that this reaction was unique to amber.

During the next two thousand years, no one fully explained what either Thales or Aristophanes had seen. Nor could they say how or why a sliver of lodestone always pointed north and south. It was clearly a useful feature, however, and led to the invention of the compass in the fourth century BCE.

Aristophanes was one of the first to note that the mineral amber contained forces of attraction. If amber is rubbed with fur or cloth, feathers will stick to the amber.

STUDYING **SCIENTIFIC DATA**

Countless wild ideas about magnets had spread by the time British physician William Gilbert carried out his experiments in the late 1500s. Some people claimed that the lodestone in a compass was affected by garlic. Many also said that magnets cured common ailments such as headaches. Gilbert lived in an era when sailors, traders, and explorers regularly journeyed from

England to locations across the globe. These travelers depended on magnetic compasses for guidance in dangerous and unfamiliar areas. Gilbert was therefore eager to collect scientific facts proving how magnets truly worked.

Gilbert used the money he earned as a doctor to fund his experiments. This marked the first time a scientist carried out controlled studies on magnets. His research lasted about seventeen years. Gilbert published a series of six books called *On the Magnet* in 1600.

Gilbert had scientifically disproved several popular theories about magnets. Yet Gilbert also suggested some new ideas of his own. For starters, heat had different effects on how lodestones and amber attract matter. He believed that these two objects produced different forces. Lodestones could be used to create magnetic force, and amber could be used to create electric force. *On the Magnet* was the first time that anyone had used the term *electric,* which is Latin for "to be like amber."

Gilbert also declared that Earth itself was a magnet! He recognized this by studying the forces of attraction between a sphere-shaped piece of lodestone and a hanging needle. The way the needle dipped as Gilbert moved it around the sphere was similar to how a compass would point toward Earth's poles. He used the term *magnetic poles* to describe the two parts of the sphere where magnetic forces seemed strongest. Gilbert saw that Earth's poles lined up with the sphere's magnetic poles. He said

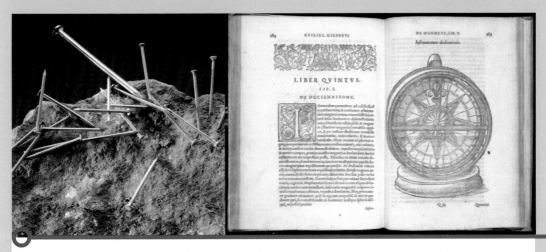

A lodestone *(left)*, also known as magnetite, attracts iron and other metals. William Gilbert's studies of the magnetic properties of lodestones gave people a scientific understanding of magnetic force. These pages from William Gilbert's *On the Magnet (right)* discuss the properties of magnetic metals. Gilbert was the first scientist to conduct controlled experiments on magnets.

this explained why a compass always pointed north and south. Thanks to Gilbert's experiments, people finally understood magnetic force.

Gilbert's work inspired others to study electric force as well. Later scientists wondered if there were other methods of generating electricity. In 1800 Italian physicist Alessandro Volta suggested that contact between two different metals would generate an electric current.

Volta tested his idea by designing a pile of alternating zinc and copper discs. The discs were separated by pieces of cloth that had been soaked in either an acid or a salt solution. By connecting wire to both ends of the pile, Volta was able to create an ongoing electric current. His invention, the electric battery, was one of the first successful attempts to generate a steady stream of electricity.

A REMARKABLE **RELATIONSHIP**

It wasn't until 1820 that scientists realized there was a connection between electricity and magnetism. That year science professor Hans Christian Ørsted prepared to show friends and students how an electric current heated a wire. In a separate demonstration, he hoped to use a compass needle to explain magnetic force. His experiments didn't stay separate for long, though! As Ørsted turned on the electric current, he suddenly noticed the compass needle was moving.

ELECTRIC AMPHIBIANS?

Volta wasn't the only Italian scientist to experiment with electricity. In 1780 Luigi Galvani had formed his own ideas about electric currents. He carried out tests using frog legs hung on metal hooks. Galvani found he could make the frog legs move by touching them with a metal probe. This led him to think he had discovered what he called "animal electricity." He believed that the frogs' muscles created an electric current. Volta was fascinated by such experiments. But he didn't agree with Galvani's conclusion. Instead, Volta realized that the frog legs were just reacting to the electricity. He suspected that the real cause of the current was the contact between the metal hooks and the probe. Volta's efforts to prove his own theory right led him to invent the electric battery.

In the days ahead, he continued to study how the magnetic needle reacted to the electric current. The current neither attracted nor repelled the needle. Instead, the needle stood perpendicular to the current. Ørsted believed that what he was seeing proved some relationship between magnetism and electricity. Yet he couldn't explain what it was.

As word of Ørsted's observations spread, other scientists worked to find the missing piece to the puzzle. French physicist and mathematician André-Marie Ampère was among this group. Ampère reasoned that Ørsted's electric current was somehow causing a magnetic force to act on the compass needle. He predicted that perhaps a similar force existed between parallel, or side-by-side, currents.

Ampère tested his theory and found a magnetic attraction between parallel wires when they carried electric currents flowing in the same direction. He also discovered a magnetic repulsion between the same wires when they carried currents flowing in opposite directions. Ampère named the relationship between electricity and magnetism "electrodynamics." Modern scientists also refer to it as electromagnetism.

The idea of electromagnetism fascinated English scientist Michael Faraday. Ampère had proven that electricity could create a magnetic field. Faraday wondered if the opposite was true too. Could magnetic force generate electricity? In 1831 Faraday connected wires to a copper disc and then spun the disc between the poles of a magnet. This motion caused a changing magnetic field. In turn, the invisible lines of magnetic force forming the field acted on the wires. The result was that a small electric current began flowing through them.

LARGE-SCALE **ELECTROMAGNETISM**

Thanks to Ampère's work, Faraday had discovered electromagnetic induction. In the decades ahead, inventors such as Thomas Edison would find new uses for this process. In the late 1870s, Edison developed one of his best-known inventions—electric lighting. Yet if he hoped to light up entire city streets, Edison needed to produce and distribute electricity on a large scale.

Faraday had proven that magnetic energy could create electrical energy. So Edison designed a generator to harness this power. His

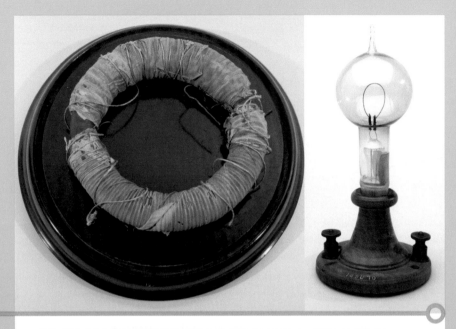

In 1831 Michael Faraday experimented with wires, a copper disc, and a magnet. The resulting electromagnetic induction ring *(left)* created a small electric current. A few decades later, Thomas Edison used elements of Faraday's experiment to design the first electric lamp *(right)*.

machine relied on a steam engine to move wire coils between two huge bipolar magnets. As Faraday had shown, this motion created an electric current.

In the summer of 1882, Edison started developing a generator plant in New York City. He installed electric lightbulbs in many of the buildings on Pearl Street. Then, on September 4, local residents and business owners watched in amazement as Edison switched on his generator. Suddenly, forty-four hundred lamps beamed electric light into 193 buildings. Edison had succeeded in using electromagnetism to deliver electricity in bulk!

The world was impressed. Yet Edison's system had its challenges. Mainly, it relied upon a direct current (DC), or a one-way electrical flow. So it was difficult to move electricity over long distances without building power stations every few miles. Ultimately, Edison's own employee proposed a solution. In 1884 Serbian engineer and inventor Nikola Tesla suggested using alternating currents (AC). Instead of just flowing one way, the currents would change direction in a series of waves.

Years earlier, Tesla had used AC currents to make a magnetic field rotate. He was convinced that a rotating magnetic field could generate AC currents in a motor. Tesla tested his ideas and put together an early model of the induction motor. Since he was using electromagnetic energy, he didn't have to rely on an outside power source such as a steam engine.

Yet Edison was unwilling to use Tesla's suggestions to change how his company produced and delivered electricity. He still supported the idea of a DC system. Eventually, the men's clashing opinions led Tesla to quit. He later sold the rights to several of his inventions—including his induction motor—to a US inventor and businessman named George Westinghouse.

Inventor Nikola Tesla came up with the idea of alternating currents (AC) to distribute electricity. Part of his role as an early proponent of electricity was to demonstrate how it worked, often with spectacular results.

THE **WAR** OF THE **CURRENTS**

The competition between Edison, Tesla, and Westinghouse wasn't always friendly. Edison earned money from companies using inventions that ran on DC power.

So Edison did his best to turn the public against AC technology. He warned them it was dangerous and unpredictable. To prove he was right, Edison used AC electricity to publicly kill stray animals. Eventually, the "War of the Currents" became even more gruesome. By 1890 people on either side of the issue debated whether to rely upon AC or DC to electrocute criminals.

The War of the Currents peaked in 1893. That year the Chicago World's Fair took place in Chicago, Illinois. Both Edison and Westinghouse were eager to power this important cultural event. In the end, however, Westinghouse said he could do the job for $155,000 less, using Tesla's AC system. During the next few years, AC electricity began to steadily overshadow DC technology. Ultimately, Edison confessed that he wished he had been more open to Tesla's suggestions.

Both Westinghouse and Edison were involved in a fierce competition to generate and distribute electricity on a large scale. In the end, AC power proved more popular. That remains true in the twenty-first century.

AN UNFINISHED **STORY**

Modern scientists continue to study electromagnetism more than a century after Edison and Tesla debated it. In 2013 people in Gumi, South Korea, began using magnetic roads to charge electric buses. Electric transportation is one method of reducing pollution caused by gas-fueled cars. Yet electric vehicles still need to be charged.

Many scientists are hopeful that magnetic roads will provide an efficient and environmentally friendly source of wireless power. If things go as planned, the new roads will allow electric vehicles to run on smaller batteries and recharge, whether they're parked or moving. Depending on how successful the bus system in Gumi becomes, electromagnetism may eventually reshape transportation all around the world. These efforts show that the story of electromagnetism is far from over.

THE SHOULDERS OF **GIANTS**

The same is true for many of the topics and timelines that shape physical science. New knowledge about everything from atoms to gravity makes future possibilities seem endless. Yet no scientific milestones have ever occurred in a vacuum. Instead, every new law or discovery is part of a much larger web. Each one is connected to ideas that can stretch back thousands of years. Major moments on the timelines of physical science happen because of all the moments that happened before them.

Isaac Newton understood this. He once declared, "If I have seen further, it is by standing on the shoulders of giants." Each of these giants had a unique story. Aristotle tutored ancient kings. Galileo was arrested for his ideas about the universe. Naturally, the giants who stood on Newton's shoulders saw even further than he did. Albert Einstein linked gravity to mind-blowing theories about time and space.

Peering ahead, it's both impossible and amazing to imagine what future scientists will be able to observe. Maybe they'll notice details that will lead them to new subatomic particles and elements. Or perhaps they'll take in the bigger picture more clearly. Scientists could develop other laws of motion or better ways to deliver electricity. Of course, no one knows for certain if or when such breakthroughs will unfold along the timelines of physical science. Yet, by standing on one another's shoulders, great thinkers will always have an astounding view of the world around them.

YOUR TURN ON THE TIMELINE

Milestones in physical science are much more than a list of dates. They are life-changing events that have a profound impact on people's day-to-day lives. Use what you have learned in this book, along with your imagination and creative writing skills, to compose a short journal entry.

First, pick one of the events listed on the timelines at the beginning of each chapter. Next, picture yourself living during that period in history. Imagine hearing about (or perhaps even witnessing!) whatever scientific breakthrough you have chosen. What effects will this new knowledge or discovery have on your life? Are you excited, scared, or in disbelief? Are you able to predict how your world will be different?

After you finish writing, consider going online or heading to your local library. See if you can find any actual first-person accounts related to the physical science milestone you selected. How do those accounts compare to your journal entry?

LERNER

Expand learning beyond the printed book. Download free, complementary educational resources for this book from our website, www.lerneresource.com.

SOURCE

SOURCE NOTES

10–11 Isaac Newton, quoted in Gerald James Holton and Stephen G. Brush, *Physics, the Human Adventure: From Copernicus to Einstein and Beyond* (Piscataway, NJ: Rutgers University, 2004), 266.

43 Isaac Newton, quoted in "Historical Figures in Astronomy," Western Washington University, accessed April 21, 2014, http://www.wwu.edu/depts/skywise/a101_historicalfigures.html.

GLOSSARY

alchemist: someone who tried to use chemical transformations to create gold, improve health, or lengthen life

bipolar magnet: a magnet that has both poles next to each other

calculus: a branch of mathematics that focuses on finding rates of change and finding measurements such as length, area, and volume

generator: a machine that changes mechanical energy into electrical energy

lodestone: a piece of magnetite or any other mineral that has naturally magnetic properties

mechanical: shaped by measurable properties and physical processes that are used to explain how forces act on matter

mineral: a solid, naturally formed substance made from nonliving matter

mystical: influenced by spiritual or supernatural forces

philosopher: a person who studies ideas about knowledge, truth, and the nature and purpose of life

quantitative: using numbers to describe or explain something

reactive: able to change chemically when something is added to it

repel: to cause objects to move away from each other

subatomic particle: an electron, neutron, proton or other tiny particle of matter that makes up an atom

theory: a statement that uses evidence to try to explain scientific facts

vacuum tube: a closed tube with all its air removed that is capable of containing a freely flowing electric current. Scientists used these to learn how electrons flowed.

SELECTED BIBLIOGRAPHY

"Antoine Lavoisier: 1743–1794." Creighton University. September 25, 2001. http://mattson.creighton.edu/History_Gas_Chemistry/Lavoisier.html.

Cohen, S. Marc, Patricia Curd, and C. D. C. Reeve, eds. *Ancient Greek Philosophy: From Thales to Aristotle.* 4th ed. Indianapolis: Hackett Publishing, 2011.

Edson, Gary. *Mysticism and Alchemy through the Ages: The Quest for Transformation.* Jefferson, NC: McFarland & Company, 2012.

"Galileo Timeline." Rice University. Accessed April 20, 2014. http://galileo.rice.edu/chron/galileo.html.

Herman, Stephen L. *Electrical Principles.* Clifton Park, NY: Delmar, 2012.

"The Periodic Table of Elements." American Institute of Physics. Accessed April 20, 2014. http://www.aip.org/history/curie/periodic.htm.

Riebeek, Holli. "Planetary Motion: The History of an Idea That Launched the Scientific Revolution." National Aeronautics and Space Administration, July 7, 2009. http://earthobservatory.nasa.gov/Features/OrbitsHistory/.

"Timeline of Electricity and Magnetism: Introduction." Florida State University. Accessed April 21, 2014. http://www.magnet.fsu.edu/education/tutorials/timeline/.

FURTHER INFORMATION

Chem4Kids.com
http://www.chem4kids.com/index.html
Visit this site for more information about matter, elements, reactions, and other chemistry basics.

Gardner, Robert. *Electricity and Magnetism Experiments Using Batteries, Bulbs, Wires, and More: One Hour or Less Science Experiments.* Berkeley Heights, NJ: Enslow Publishers, 2013. Check out this book for ideas for cool experiments related to electricity, magnetism, and electromagnetism!

The Human Touch of Chemistry—Periodic Table
http://humantouchofchemistry.com/periodic-table.htm#
Go to this site to explore an interactive version of the periodic table of elements.

McPherson, Stephanie Sammartino. *War of the Currents: Thomas Edison vs. Nikola Tesla.* Minneapolis: Twenty-First Century Books, 2013. Read this book for more details on the scientific developments and competitive back story that fueled the AC/DC debate.

Miller, Ron. *Recentering the Universe: The Radical Theories of Copernicus, Kepler, Galileo, and Newton.* Minneapolis: Twenty-First Century Books, 2014. Take a closer look at how scientists built upon one another's ideas to retool people's understanding of physics and the universe.

INDEX

alchemy, 4, 16, 18–19
Alexander the Great, 8, 10
Ampère, André-Marie, 35, 39
Aristophanes, 34, 36
Aristotle, 6, 8–10, 19, 26, 28–30, 43
astronomy, 31
atomic bombs, 15
atomic mass (atomic weight), 13, 17, 21–22, 24
atomic numbers, 13, 25
atoms (*atomos*), 7, 8–9, 11–15, 21, 23–24

books on physical science: *On the Magnet* (Gilbert) , 34, 37; *The Principles of Philosophy* (Descartes), 10
Boyle, Robert, 16, 19–20

Chadwick, James, 7, 14–15
chemistry: in the fourth century BCE, 18; in the 1600s, 19; in the 1700s, 20–21; in the 1800s, 21–23; in the 1900s, 24–25
chemists, 19, 21
compounds, 11, 21
Curie, Marie Sklodowska, 17, 22–25
Curie, Pierre, 17, 22–25

Dalton, John, 7, 11–12
Democritus, 6, 8–11
Descartes, René, 6, 10

Edison, Thomas, 35, 39–48
Einstein, Albert, 27, 32, 43
electricity, 34–35; alternating current (AC), 35–36, 41–42; direct current (DC), 35–36, 40–42
electromagnetism, 35, 36, 39, 42–43
elements, 8, 11, 13, 17, 19–25, 28
Empedocles, 6, 8–9, 28
experiments: alchemy experiments, 4, 18; Boyle's gas experiment, 19; Chadwick's radiation experiment, 14; Curie's radium experiment, 25; Dalton's gas experiments, 11; Faraday's electromagnetic induction experiment, 35, 40; fiber-optic cable experiments, 33; Galileo's experiments on motion, 29–30; Gilbert's magnet experiments, 36–37; Lavoisier's chemical reaction experiment, 20; Ørsted's electromagnetic experiments, 38–39; Rutherford's gold foil experiment, 12; Thomson's cathode-ray tube experiment, 12

Faraday, Michael, 35, 39–40

Galilei, Galileo, 26, 29–30, 43
Galvani, Luigi, 38
geometry, 10
Gilbert, William, 34, 36–38

hypothesis, 4

inertia, 30, 32
inventions, 12, 36, 38, 39–41

Lavoisier, Antoine-Laurent, 17, 20–21
Lavoisier, Marie, 21
law of conservation of mass, 20
Leucippus, 9

magnets, 34–35, 36–37
mass, 10–11, 20, 31–32
matter, 6, 9, 14–15, 18–19, 20, 28
Mendeleev, Dmitri, 17, 21–22
Moseley, Henry, 24–25
motion: Aristotle's rules of, 26, 28; Newton's laws of, 27, 30–31, 33; theories on, 28

Newton, Isaac, 6, 10–11, 27, 30–33, 43
nuclear energy, 15

Ørsted, Hans Christian, 35, 38–39

periodic table of elements, 17, 22–25
philosophers, 8–10, 19, 36
philosophy; in ancient Greece, 8–10; in the 1800s, 11; in the 1900s, 12–14; in the 1600s, 10

PHOTO ACKNOWLEDGMENTS

The images in this book are used with the permission of: © Ancient Art and Architecture Collection Ltd/ Bridgeman Images, p. 5; © Bibliotheque Mazarine, Paris, France/Archives Charmet/Bridgeman Images, pp. 6 (top), 8; © Album/Oronoz/Album/SuperStock, pp. 6 (center), 10; © Christie's Images Ltd/SuperStock, p. 6 (bottom); © Science and Society/ SuperStock, pp. 7 (top left), 13 (top, bottom), 16 (left), 18 (right); © Science Source, pp. 7 (bottom left), 9, 11, 17 (top right), 26 (right); © Dorling Kindersley/Vetta/Getty Images, pp. 7 (top right), 14; © SPL/Science Source, pp. 7 (bottom right), 15; © Devonshire Collection, Chatsworth/Reproduced by permission of Chatsworth Settlement Trustees/Bridgeman Images, p. 16 (right); © Sovfoto/UIG via Getty Images, pp. 17 (top left), 22 (right); © The Metropolitan Museum of Art, pp. 17 (bottom left), 21; © Iberfoto/SuperStock, pp. 17 (bottom right), 20, 23; © Zev Radovan/Bridgeman Images, p. 18 (left); © Fine Art Images/SuperStock, p. 22 (left); © Private Collection/Bridgeman Images, p. 24 (top); © Pantheon/SuperStock, p. 24 (bottom); © Royal Astronomical Society/Science Source, p. 26 (top); © Look and Learn/Bridgeman Images, pp. 26 (bottom left), 29, 35 (bottom left); National Maritime Museum/Wikimedia Commons, p. 27 (left); © British Library/Robana via Getty Images, p. 27 (middle); © koya979/Deposit Photos, pp. 27 (right), 32; © Jean-Leon Huens/National Geographic Creative/Bridgeman Images, p. 30; NASA/Joel Kowsky, p. 33; © Dorling Kindersley/UIG/Bridgeman Images, pp. 34 (top), 36; © The Stapleton Collection/Bridgeman Images, pp. 34 (bottom left), 37 (right); © The Royal Institution, London, UK/Bridgeman Images, pp. 34 (right), 35 (top left), 40 (left); © Science Museum, London, UK/Bridgeman Images, pp. 35 (top right), 40 (right); © Everett Collection/SuperStock, pp. 35 (bottom right), 41; © De Agostini Picture Library/Photo 1/Getty Images, p. 37 (left); © Chicago History Museum/Getty Images, p. 42; © iStockphoto.com/Cesare Ferrari, (light burst).

Front cover: © Ted Kinsman/Photo Researchers/Getty Images.